Engineering the

Dream. Create. Engineer!

~Patty
O'Brien Novak
2011

How Engineers
Shape Our World

by Patty O'Brien Novak
illustrations by Don McLean

FERNE PRESS

Engineering the ABCs: How Engineers Shape our World

Copyright © 2010 by Patty O'Brien Novak

Illustrated by Don McLean

Layout and cover design by Kimberly Franzen and Raphael Giuffrida

Printed in Canada

Summary: From A to Z, this book provides child-friendly examples of how engineers shape our world.

Library of Congress Cataloging-in-Publication Data

O'Brien Novak, Patty
Engineering the ABCs: How Engineers Shape Our World / Patty O'Brien Novak – First Edition
ISBN-13: 978-1-933916-51-4
Engineering the ABCs: How Engineers Shape our World
1. Engineering 2. Alphabet 3. Children 4. Technology 5. Science
I. O'Brien Novak, Patty II. Engineering the ABCs: How Engineers Shape our World
Library of Congress Control Number: 2009937217

FERNE PRESS

Ferne Press is an imprint of Nelson Publishing & Marketing
366 Welch Road, Northville, MI 48167
www.nelsonpublishingandmarketing.com
(248) 735-0418

To Anna, my loving daughter and book writing bud; Drew, my "real facts" son and the inspiration for this book; and Rob, my husband and loyal supporter.

Special thank you to the Detroit Section of the Society of Women Engineers for their support. (www.swedetroit.org)

SWE

Society of
Women Engineers

ASPIRE · ADVANCE · ACHIEVE

Why are airplane wings so big?

Wings help airplanes soar through the air, and these planes are very heavy. Bigger airplanes weigh over 600,000 lbs (275,000 kg)! Engineers use special computer programs to create wings that can lift the weight of the airplane, plus the weight of passengers, fuel, and cargo.

airplane

Airplane flights in the 1920s were guided for landing by bonfires and beacons.

See answer on page 30.

Some airplane wings are over 250 feet (76 m) wide. If the average school bus is 40 feet (12 m) long, how many school buses could be placed in a line on the wing?

A. 3 buses   B. 6 buses   C. 11 buses

Let's Discover...

4

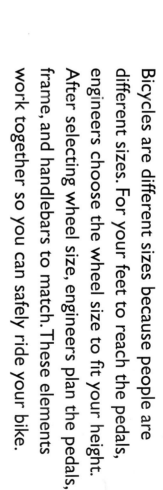

Why are bicycles different sizes?

bicycle

Bicycles are different sizes because people are different sizes. For your feet to reach the pedals, engineers choose the wheel size to fit your height. After selecting wheel size, engineers plan the pedals, frame, and handlebars to match. These elements work together so you can safely ride your bike.

Engineering students developed a bicycle that glows in the dark by applying current technology in a new way. On the bicycle frame, the students used light panels from glow-in-the-dark wristwatches.

What makes a car go?

A car's engine produces power by mixing gas and air in the piston chamber. This power moves gears, which turn the wheels to make your car go. All this is done by engineers programming a small computer before it is placed near your car's engine.

C car

XING

The first cars had no roof, no music player, no air conditioning, no heat, no computers, and were very expensive. In 1908, Henry Ford introduced the first affordable car, known as the Model T, which was made possible through a well-crafted mass production system.

Let's Discover...

dolls

How are dolls made?

Dolls can be made by hand to produce a few or by machine to produce thousands. The machines use "molds," or shaped pans, to form the doll's head, body, and arms. Engineers design these machines and molds.

Before the 1800s, most dolls were handmade from wood. Since the 1950s, most dolls have been machine-made from vinyl. The handmade process can take days to make one doll, while the machine-made process can make a doll in minutes.

You can tour some doll-making factories. Visit www.factorytoursusa.com for more information.

Where does electricity come from?

electricity

Electricity is the flow of electrical charge from one atom to another. It comes from many sources—wind, water, coal, oil, sunlight, and even uranium. Power stations make the electricity for most homes. Engineers working in these power stations keep large turbines and generators operating to produce electricity.

Using solar panels or windmills, homes can be designed as small power stations. They can take energy from the sun or wind to power the home's lights, computers, refrigerator, and even the television.

See answer on page 30.

Let's Discover...

How many volts of electricity does a personal computer use?

A. 3,276 volts   B. 15 volts   C. 110 volts

How does all this food get here?

Some grocery stores buy lots of food for their many stores across the country. The food is delivered to a central warehouse. Then the warehouse needs help getting the food out to each store. Engineers identify the most efficient routes to use. Engineers look for paths that save money on gas for the trucks while still getting the food to each store as quickly as possible.

The first self-service grocery store opened in the United States in 1916. Before this, grocery stores were much smaller with no shopping carts. There were just a few shelves, and clerks did the shopping for you.

How is a video game made?

Anyone can write the idea for a video game. When the story is approved for use, engineers program the code controlling how the game plays. One of the last steps is testing the game. By the time a new video game reaches store shelves, engineers have tested the software over 100 times to ensure the game will operate as intended.

games

In the 1940s, engineers discovered that a moth had crawled into their test computer, causing malfunctions. It was the first case of an actual bug causing a computer bug!

GAME TECH

Ralph Baer was one of the first inventors of home video game systems. His engineering work led to the creation of Odyssey, the first home video game. In what year was Odyssey released?

A. 1972   B. 1902   C. 1999

See answer on page 30.

Let's Discover...

How can a helmet protect my head?

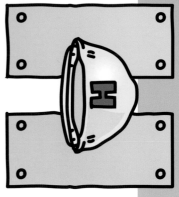

helmet

Kids and adults wear helmets to protect their heads from injury. The helmet absorbs the shock of collisions. Engineers develop strong, lightweight materials for these helmets and conduct a series of tests to check their strength. One type of test is dropping helmets from very tall buildings.

Different helmets are needed for different activities because the impacts to the helmet can be very different. If the activity, such as football, takes place on turf, the helmet must protect against many repeated softer impacts. However, if the activity takes place on concrete as in bike riding, the helmet must protect against one or two hard impacts. Can you name other activities where helmets are required?

11

What makes ice cream so creamy?

ice cream

Making cream from ice, milk, and salt requires lots of mixing. Machines slowly stir the icy mixture as it cools. Slow stirring creates a creamy texture by preventing large ice crystals from forming. Engineers design machines that mix and pour the ice cream into brightly colored containers.

During the 1904 World's Fair, an ice cream maker ran out of bowls to serve his ice cream. He asked a nearby waffle maker to roll waffles into cones to hold the ice cream. This was the invention of the ice cream cone.

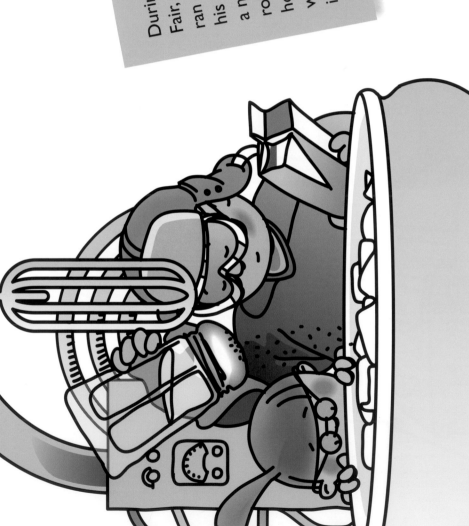

Let's Discover...

The most popular ice cream flavor in the United States is

A. Butter Pecan   B. Vanilla   C. Strawberry

See answer on page 30.

jeans

How are my jeans made?

The jeans you wear are made from white cotton fibers woven into denim cloth. After that, the traditional blue color is added. Engineers make special machines to cut the cloth into pockets, belt loops, and the other pieces needed to assemble a pair of jeans. These special machines can cut through 100 layers of cloth at one time! After the cloth is cut, the material is sewn together at the seams and ready for wearing.

Recycled blue jeans are becoming a popular insulation material for houses. The fibers from the blue jeans make the insulation soft and easy to handle. This material is also known as natural cotton batt insulation.

Although the first denim pants date back to the 1500s in Italy, Levi Strauss was one of the first Americans to sell jeans in the United States. If you were buying jeans in the 1880s, how much money would you have paid Mr. Strauss for a pair of jeans?

A. $20   B. $0.05   C. $1.50

See answer on page 30.

What makes a kite fly?

A kite flies because a thin material stretched across rods catches the wind, lifting it into the sky. Many different materials, such as paper, silk, and even steel, can be used to build a kite, but engineers look for materials that will stretch without tearing yet are light enough so the kite floats.

kite

In World War I, before airplanes were common, kites were used for enemy observation and signaling.

According to archeological studies, people living on the islands of Fiji originally built kites to catch fish. From the shore, the kites were used to cast fishing lines out into deeper waters where more fish were swimming.

Let's
Discover...

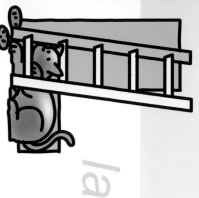

ladder

How does a ladder help us?

A ladder helps us reach high places like a roof, an attic, or even a bunk bed. Engineers research materials and step, or rung, design to develop ladders that are light enough to carry around our homes, but will not break under heavy loads.

Fire truck ladders rescue people from high buildings and can reach 100 feet in the air. If one story of a building is 12 feet high, how many stories can a ladder truck reach?

A. 263 stories   B. 8 stories   C. 2 stories

See answer on page 30.

How are cameras used to make a movie?

A crew uses many cameras to record the movie's actions, also called scenes, onto film or computer. Engineers design and build these cameras. Sometimes engineers plan the special effects and fabricate the elaborate movie sets as well.

Movies

ENGINEERING THE ABC's

TAKE 1

Making people or objects fly is important to the storyline of many movies. Much of this flying is done by special computer software that makes these things look like they are flying.

How do noodles get their shape?

First, flour and water are mixed together to form a dough. Then the dough is pushed through a metal disc with holes in it. This metal disc is called a die. Engineers design the dies that give noodles their unique sizes and shapes: round, curly, flat, wavy, large, and small.

Archeologists discovered well-preserved noodles under an earthenware bowl in China. These noodles are over 4,000 years old!

Noodles can also be made by hand. All you need are the ingredients, a rolling pin, and lots of time. Start by rolling the dough into very thin sheets and then use a knife to cut the shape you want.

Why doesn't an oven melt?

The inside of an oven gets very hot, yet it does not melt. Engineers conduct tests to identify materials suited for high temperatures. These materials include cast iron, stainless steel, and porcelain. Sometimes they even invent new types of materials, such as composites, or blends, of nickel and chrome.

oven

Many types of ovens exist for cooking many types of food. These ovens include clay, wood, coal, convection, steam, microwave, and even solar.

In 1947, the first microwave oven stood 5 ½ feet tall and weighed more than 750 lbs—about the size of some refrigerators!

Let's Discover...

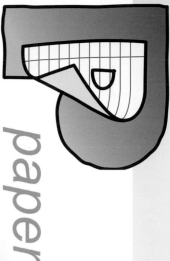

How is paper made?

Paper can be made from plants, trees, linen, straw, grasses, and even recycled papers. Machines mix these materials into a slushy pulp, and then engineers set up processes to convert the pulp into thin sheets of paper.

Estimates show that one ton of recycled paper saves 3.3 cubic yards of landfill space—about the size of your bedroom closet. What steps can you take to recycle?

Beautiful pop-up books require a combination of creativity, artistry, and engineering to manipulate ordinary paper into intricate, movable shapes that "pop" out of the book. Pop-up books have been around for over 500 years.

How are quarters made?

Quarters start as thin sheets of metal. These sheets are fed through a machine that punches out blank metal circles. After these blank discs are washed and dried, the last step is the coining press, which strikes the picture, the value, and the motto onto both sides. The engineering team at the US Mint chooses these machines and presses.

quarters

A quarter is worth $0.25. How many quarters are needed to make $2.25?

A. 9 quarters   B. 7 quarters   C. 18 quarters

See answer on page 30.

Let's Discover...

rocket

How do rockets get into space?

3-2-1.... BLAST OFF! Rocket engines burn lots of fuel to make tons of force. This force lifts a rocket off the earth and propels it into space. Engineers design rocket engines to withstand high heat and pressure.

Engineers from several companies and NASA are working on building a cable for a space elevator that could transport humans 62,000 miles (100,000 km) into space!

Sally Ride became the first American woman in space with her 1983 space shuttle mission. To become an astronaut, you need a college degree in engineering, math, or science.

21

How does a stethoscope work?

stethoscope

Medical workers use a stethoscope to listen to your heart, lungs, and other sounds inside your body. Stethoscopes focus on your heart, lungs, and abdomen while blocking out all other noises. Engineers select materials and electronics that are best suited for blocking out unwanted sounds, such as people talking, babies crying, or even the traffic noises that paramedics often encounter.

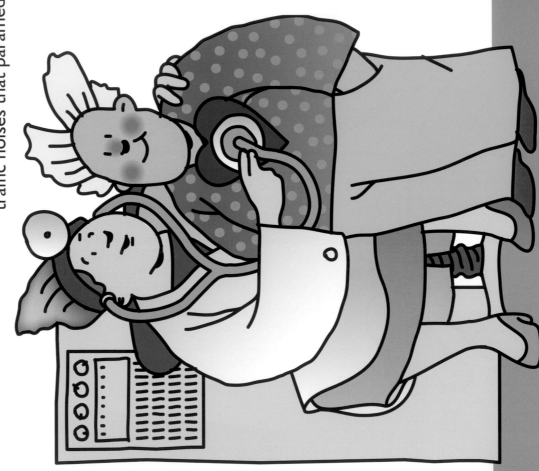

The stethoscope was invented in 1816 by French physician René Laënnec. He was inspired by young children who were scratching a pin on a wooden beam and listening to its sound being passed along the length of the beam.

Let's
Discover...

22

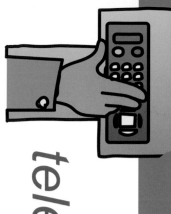

How does a television work?

A television converts electrical signals into images and sounds on a screen. Engineers research different materials to learn which ones provide the best picture and sound quality.

television

The 1954 New Year's Day Tournament of Roses Parade was the first television program seen in color. Before then, television shows were in black and white.

Some of the first television sets came with a tiny three-inch viewing screen. There were just a few channels, no sound, and no remote control. In what year did the modern TV remote control become widely available?

A. 1927   B. 1880   C. 1980

See answer on page 30.

23

How do umbrellas open?

When you open your umbrella, the slider pushes thin metal rods up and out. These rods work together with special fabric to create a canopy over our heads. Engineers devise these rods to glide open without breaking. This is not an easy task, as thin metal can be very brittle.

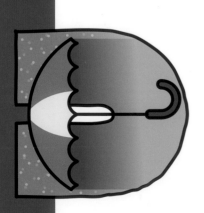

umbrella

Umbrellas have been used for thousands of years. In ancient China, India, and the Middle East, umbrellas were often a symbol of royalty and honor. Bumbershoot is another name for umbrella. Americans used the term over two hundred years ago and some still do today.

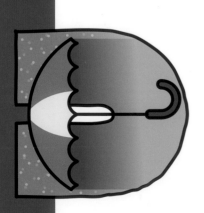*Let's*
Discover...

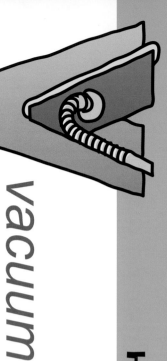

vacuum

How does a vacuum cleaner work?

Vacuum cleaners create suction to pick up dirt from floors. This suction happens through the use of pumps and motors. Engineers construct these pumps and motors to be small and light, so cleaning your floors is quick and easy.

Some of the first vacuum cleaners were difficult to operate, because you had to turn a crank with one hand while pushing the vacuum across the floor with the other hand.

In 1905, the first portable vacuum cleaner weighed a whopping 92 lbs (42 kg) and did not sell well. Three years later, engineers removed over half the weight to produce a better selling device weighing in at 40 lbs (18 kg).

How does water get to our house?

In some parts of the world, people get water by dipping a bucket into a stream. And in other parts of the world, people get water from the faucets in their homes. Water to homes is delivered through a massive network of underground pipes, tunnels, and valves. From choosing the pipe size, to developing stronger materials, to inventing new ways to clean the water, engineers work on just about every part of the water delivery system.

water

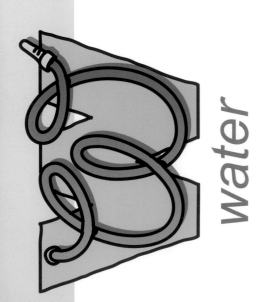

Water is a limited, natural resource and engineers are working on new methods to clean our water for reuse. What are some things you can do to reduce the amount of water your family or school uses? Can you think of ways to reuse water?

The Hoover Dam in southern Nevada is one of the United States' largest water management projects. The dam supplies water to cities over 300 miles away, generates electricity for 750,000 people, and stops damaging floods from occurring.

xylophone

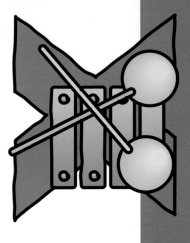

How does a xylophone make music?

A xylophone is made of different sized bars which are placed on a frame. The larger bars produce a lower sound than the smaller bars. When you strike a series of bars with a hard mallet, you make music. Engineers design the frame that holds the xylophone, making it lightweight for easy transport.

Children and adults around the world play many different types of xylophones. These instruments can vary in size, and in number and type of bars. There is even one xylophone that is twelve feet long and can be played by up to six people.

How is yarn made?

Yarn is a long strand of connected fibers. These fibers can be natural (cotton, flax, silk, and wool) or synthetic (rayon, nylon, and polyester). Spinning machines twist these fibers into long strands. Engineers build these machines that spin the colorful threads into rainbows of yarn.

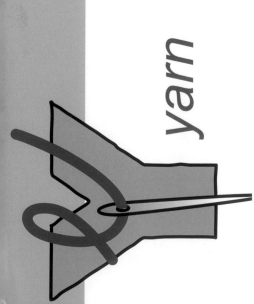

yarn

Cotton has been used to make fabrics for at least 7,000 years.

In Guatemala, Mayan women use a hand loom every day to weave all sorts of things for their families, such as blankets, shirts, dresses, and many other items. It can take two to three months to weave a traditional huipil, a blouse worn by the village women.

How does a zipper work?

A zipper has dozens of teeth that are exactly the same shape and size. These teeth come together when you pull up your zipper. Although a zipper looks simple, making one requires high-tech equipment. Engineers monitor the manufacturing equipment to ensure that the millions of teeth made are all identical.

Early names for the zipper included "C-curity Fastener," "Separable Fastener," "Hookless Fastener," and "Clasp Locker." Early uses for the zipper included fastening soldiers' flying suits, life vests, and money belts during World War I.

Let's Discover...

In 1917, Gideon Sundback patented his idea for a zipper, which was used primarily on boots. Buttons were still used on clothing. How many years do you think passed before the zipper became popular in clothing?

A. 3 years   B. 20 years   C. 75 years

See answer on page 30.

Note to Parents/Educators/Librarians:

One day my son proclaimed, "Engineers do not build the space shuttle, scientists do!" How could my young son have no idea what engineers do? After all, he was being raised by two engineers. I am a mechanical engineer and my husband is an electrical engineer.

However, when I started looking at his books, television shows, and videos, I realized that engineers were rarely mentioned. Instead they spoke of scientists. But engineers and scientists are not the same. Scientists develop the theories and engineers apply the theories.

Engineers breathe life into ideas and make them reality. For example, the idea for cellular communications was generated in the 1940s. However, mobile phones did not become a reality until engineers produced microelectronic components and integrated circuits in the 1970s.

When children hear the word "engineer," I want them to think of more than someone who drives a train. I want them to think of things like zippers, cars, and even ice cream! Engineering relates to so many parts of a child's everyday life. Saying simple things to children, like "Engineers had a part in making this chair, or this pencil, or this book," will help them understand how engineers shape their world.

I wish you well in exploring engineering with your child.

Patty O'Brien Novak

Answers to Let's Discover:

Page 4: B. 6 buses
Page 12: B. Vanilla
Page 20: A. 9 quarters

Page 8: C. 110 volts
Page 13: C. $1.50
Page 23: C. 1980

Page 10: A. 1972
Page 15: B. 8 stories
Page 29: B. 20 years

About the Author

Patty O'Brien Novak received her BS in Mechanical Engineering from the University of Cincinnati. Her previous work experience includes eleven years as an engineer in Ford Motor Company's Powertrain group and two years as an engineering co-op with Cincinnati Milacron.

Patty's passion for engineering and explaining, in simple terms, how things work is contagious. She loves teaching children, through presentations, books and experiments, about the incredible impact engineers have on their daily world. Patty enjoys her current position of domestic engineer, managing the daily activities of her family. She lives in Michigan with her husband, Rob, and her two children, Drew and Anna.

To learn more about the author and school visits, visit www.PattyOBrienNovak.com.

About the Illustrator

Don McLean has been illustrating and designing for over forty years. He started in 1969 at a large commercial art studio in Detroit, Michigan. In 1976, Don opened his own studio, McLean and Friends, employing as many as thirty-five artists of varying illustrative styles and techniques. He is now the founder of www.yourmemorylane.com, another group of artists that interprets life's memories into graphic images for a unique story-telling Memory Lane gift.

Illustrating a children's book has been a long time dream of Don's and illustrating Engineering the ABCs has totally fulfilled his expectations.

"I've enjoyed the creative approach to explaining the possibilities of the profession of an engineer. Decorative illustration is a universal way to communicate with children."

Don resides in Farmington Hills, Michigan.

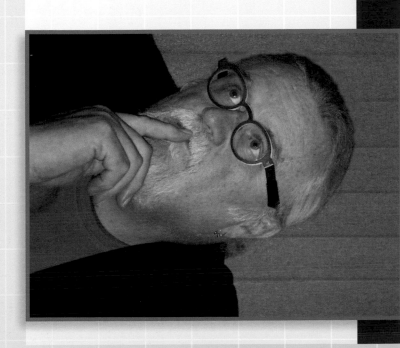